Exploring Caves

Written by Jenny Feely

Series Consultant: Linda Hoyt

WorldWise™
Content-based Learning

T0360036

Contents

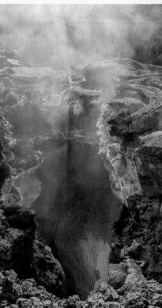

Introduction

Under the ground there are open spaces, parts of which never receive direct sunlight. They are caves. In them, you might find incredible rock formations, **fossils** of plants and animals, or art that is thousands of years old.

Caves are found all over the world. They can be small and close to the ground's surface, or huge and run deep underground. People and animals have lived in or visited caves for thousands of years.

Mammoth–Flint Ridge Cave System in Kentucky, United States, is the longest known cave system in the world, with more than 600 kilometres explored.

The largest cave room discovered is called the Big Room. It is in the Carlsbad Caverns in the Guadalupe Mountains of southeastern New Mexico in the United States. It measures almost 1,200 metres long, 190 metres wide, and 77 metres high at its highest point.

Caves are a rich source of information for scientists to learn about Earth's history. They provide information on how caves were formed and what people and animals lived in them.

There must be a huge number of caves that have never been found or explored, so there is much more history for scientists to discover.

Chapter 1

How are caves formed?

Caves can be formed in different ways – by the force of moving water or ice, by movements in Earth's crust or by the power of the wind.

Mighty water

Many caves are formed by water. Underground rivers, that flow through the earth, wear away rock and leave behind tunnels and caves.

Above the ground, caves along the shores of oceans or lakes are formed over time by wave action.

Caves formed by melting ice are found on **glaciers**.

Limestone caves

Limestone caves are among the most spectacular of any caves under the earth. Limestone is a rock that dissolves easily over time. Limestone caves are formed when rainwater, which has traces of acid, drips through cracks in the limestone and dissolves the rocks. Over a long period of time, the water carves out larger holes that become caves.

Sea caves

Sea caves are formed by waves, as they wear away the rock at the base of cliffs. Sometimes the rock at the base of a cliff is softer than the surrounding rock or there is a crack in the rock. As the waves hit the rock over and over again, small grains of the rock are broken off and washed away. Eventually, a cave forms.

Blowholes

Sometimes the roof of a sea cave collapses and a blowhole is formed. When large waves rush into the cave, the water can explode up through the hole in the rock as if being blown out of the cave. This is how blowholes got their name.

Did you know?
Caves can be formed in deserts. This usually happens where strong winds blow into cracks in sandstone cliffs. The sandstone is worn away and caves are formed.

7

The moving earth

The earth's surface is made of gigantic plates of rock, which are constantly moving under the continents or oceans. As the plates move, they tend to slide under or over the edge of the plate next to them. Movements and changes in the earth's crust often form caves.

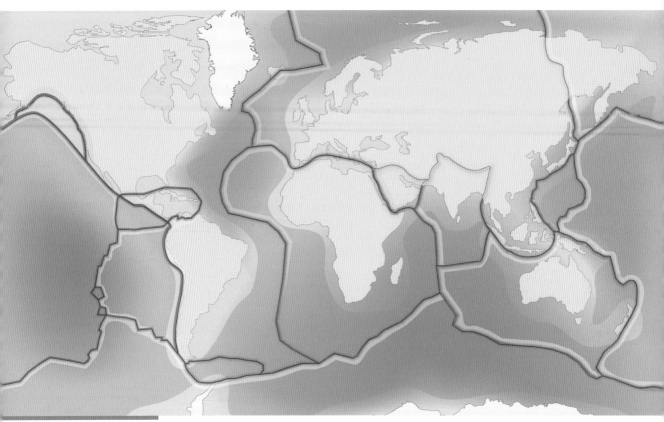

The lines on this map show Earth's plates.

Earthquakes

Sometimes the movement of the earth's plates causes earthquakes. The earth cracks, and the ground can split open and form a cave.

When an earthquake subsides, a space can be left in the ground and a cave is formed. These caves are an excellent place to study geology. The walls, ceiling and floor can show how the ground has been bent or fractured by movements in the earth's crust. The type of rock that is found can be studied without having to dig deep into the earth.

The view from inside a lava tube cave

Lava caves

Caves can also be created after a volcano has erupted.

When volcanoes erupt, rivers of **molten** rock, called lava, flow over the land. Air cools the lava, and the top layer becomes solid. Underneath this solid top layer, molten lava continues to flow. It, too, eventually cools and stops flowing. Now, there are two layers of lava with a gap in between. This gap between the layers can become an underground tunnel or cave.

Did you know?

Tunnels formed by lava are called lava tubes. The longest and deepest lava tube in the world is the Kazumura Cave in Hawaii. It is about 65 kilometres long and 1,100 metres deep.

9

Chapter 2

People living in caves

People have lived in caves for thousands of years. There were very good reasons for this.

Caves provide shelter from the weather and from the climate. Under the ground, the temperature remains much the same no matter what time of day or what season. The temperature stays around a comfortable 20 degrees Celsius.

Often caves are hidden from view, which provided protection for the people sheltering in them. Scientists study caves to learn about the past.

Think about ...

Almost one-third of known early human **fossils** have been found in caves. What other things from the past could scientists find in caves?

An ancient stone tool.

Earliest known cave people

The remains of early cave dwellers have remained in caves for hundreds and thousands of years. Studying the bones and tools found in the caves gives us insight into how the first humans may have lived.

Grotte du Vallonnet – France

More than 100 stone tools, dated to over one million years old, have been found in a cave called the Grotte du Vallonnet in France. These tools were made by early humans and were used to cut things or to pound and break things. The people who made these tools probably did not live in the cave, but they may have taken shelter there when needed.

Grotte du Vallonnet

Zhoukoudian – China

The ancient remains of 45 people, as well as some tools they used for hunting and making things, have been discovered in the caves of Zhoukoudian, near Beijing in China. The presence of so many skeletons in the cave suggests that these people lived in the caves for at least some part of the year. This group of people has been called Peking Man.

Zhoukoudian

Human remains and tools between 200 and 500 thousand years old were discovered at Zhoukoudian, China, in 1929.

Cave paintings

Ancient artwork has been found on the ceilings and walls of some caves. People in the past used strongly coloured clay to paint these pictures. This art can tell us about the lives of people who lived thousands of years ago.

No one knows exactly why the people who left these paintings chose to paint them.

The earliest cave paintings found are more than 40,000 years old. They show miniature buffaloes, warty pigs and human hands. They were found in a cave in the tropical forests of Sulawesi, in Indonesia.

Sulawesi cave art with hand prints.

A system of caves in Lascaux, France, is famous for its **prehistoric** pictures of horses, stags and bulls. The caves contain more than 2,000 images that are estimated to be about 20,000 years old.

Cave pictures that are 20,000 years old in Lascaux, France

Kakadu rock art

Kakadu National Park is a UNESCO World Heritage site and an important reason for this is that it is home to some of the world's greatest rock art sites. Some pictures have been found in caves that are nearly 20,000 years old. They provide a record of Aboriginal life showing how people lived through changing times and their interaction with the environment. The paintings often describe ancestral spirits, animals that were hunted for food or objects that were used in their daily life.

Modern cave dwellers

Many people still live in caves today. The caves are very comfortable and provide protection from extreme weather conditions.

Turkey

Cappadocia

Cappadocia, in Turkey, is a landscape formed by volcanic eruptions that threw huge amounts of ash into the air. When this ash settled on the ground, it formed a thick layer of soft rock. Over time, the softest parts of the rock were worn away by the wind and the rain leaving towers, called fairy chimneys, rising above the ground and caves under the ground.

People first settled in Cappadocia nearly 4,000 years ago to protect themselves from the freezing winters and extremely hot summers. It was a safe place to hide from warring armies that invaded Turkey from time to time. They extended the natural caves by digging new tunnels. An underground city provided a home for thousands of people.

A cave hotel in Cappadocia, Turkey

A bedroom inside the cave hotel

Over time, more and more chambers were dug to serve as homes, stables and even schools. The people dug narrow shafts up through the rock to let in air and light. These were dug at an angle to stop rain and wind from getting in.

Today, many people still live in the caves. The area is also a popular tourist destination as it has unique geological, historic and cultural features. Tourists can also stay in some of these caves.

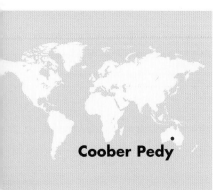

Coober Pedy

Australia

Coober Pedy is an opal-mining town in **outback** Australia with a population of almost 2,000 people. The desert temperatures can reach more than 45 degrees Celsius during the day, so to escape the heat many people have houses under the ground. They are called dugouts.

In these houses the temperature is always comfortable, and light and air come in through **ventilation** shafts. These houses also have electric power and running water. Some even have gyms and swimming pools.

China

Yaodongs are house caves in northern China. They are made by digging into the soft earth and rock of hillsides and cliffs to make rooms. The entrance to these rooms is then bricked up to provide a front wall. It is thought that more than 40 million people live in *yaodongs*. People have been digging out and living in *yaodongs* for more than 2,000 years.

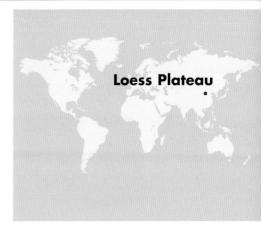

Loess Plateau

Chapter 3

Animals living in caves

Evidence from the past

Fossils

A **fossil** is the remains or the impression of the remains of an animal or plant that once lived. Fossils can be the bones of an animal, the remains of plants and animals that have become **petrified** and turned into rock, or impressions, such as footprints.

Fossils tell us what animals and plants looked like and how they lived thousands of years ago.

Fossils can be found in many places, but caves are very good places to find them. Many caves have not been visited by people or animals, so the fossils that are found in caves have often remained undisturbed. Also, the temperature inside a cave usually remains the same, which helps preserve fossils over a long period of time.

Some of the best-preserved fossils are found in limestone caves, and well-preserved fossils have been found in underwater caves.

Animals living in caves today

Caves are homes for many animals. They provide shelter from the weather and hiding places from **predators**. They are also good places to find or store food.

Animals use caves for many reasons and some do not live in caves all of the time. Bears use caves to hibernate during winter, sleeping safely out of the cold until spring comes.

There are other animals that spend all of their lives in caves – they never leave them and they adapt to their cave environment. Cave spiders live only in caves, stringing their webs in the darkness waiting to catch unwary insects that happen by.

And for some animals like bats, caves provide a resting place and a safe haven for their young.

Some animals that use caves

Cave spiders	Snakes	Bats
Live in caves permanently	Live in or near caves to find food	Shelter in caves

The cave gudgeon is a blind fish found in Western Australia. This fish lives its entire life in dark limestone pools in caves along the coast. It has no eyes and relies on sensory organs on its head to navigate and to find food. The cave gudgeon has no colour or pigment in its skin.

Bears	Salamanders	Pikas
Hibernate in caves	May be found in caves	Store food in caves

Conclusion

It is likely that many caves are yet to be discovered or explored. Some are deep underwater or below the ground and difficult to get to. Some will be found only after movement of the earth opens them to light.

The action of water, wind and ice continues to carve out new caves and reveal older ones.

These caves may be places of amazing beauty or rare historical significance, or simply a place that provided shelter for people or animals.

As these caves are discovered, new and interesting ideas and opportunities will be unlocked.

Glossary

fossils prehistoric animal or plant remains that have been in the ground for a long time

glaciers slow-moving river of ice

molten melted by heat

navigate to find the way to a place

outback remote part of Australia, far from cities

petrified something that has changed into stone over a long time

pigment a substance that gives colour to animals and plants

predators animals that hunt other animals for food

prehistoric in the time before people could write

ventilation to allow fresh air to move through a place

Index